The Time-Saving dad:
How to Juggle a Lot, Enjoy Your Life, and Accomplish What Matters Most

James D. Greene

All rights reserved. No part of this publication may be reproduced, distributed, or transmitted in any form or by any means, including photocopying, recording, or other electronic or mechanical methods, without the prior written permission of the publisher, except in the case of brief quotations embodied in critical reviews and certain other noncommercial uses permitted by copyright law.

Copyright © James D. Greene, 2022.

Table of contents

[Chapter 1](#)
[Chapter 2](#)
[Chapter 3](#)
[Chapter 4](#)
[Chapter 5](#)
[Chapter 6](#)

Chapter 1

How to manage your time and your life

Time Management Tips for Achieving Your Goals

One of the most useful abilities you may have in life is strong and efficient time management.
If you're not managing your time properly, there's no way you're going to meet your objectives at work and the life outside of it.
Sure, you may make some progress.
But your time management will be an uphill struggle if you don't treat your time seriously.
For individuals who squander and waste the very little time they do have, they know all too well how tough reaching even somewhat challenging objectives can be.

The fact is that time is the greatest equalizer in life.
No matter who you are, your age, income, gender, color, or religion, you have the same amount of time as the next person.

Whether you're fabulously wealthy or dirt poor, your time is the same.
It's not about how much time you have.
It's about how successfully you manage your time.

So if you're serious about accomplishing your objectives, not only do you need to establish those goals properly, but you also have to become serious about avoiding distractions and being too entrenched in the bad habits that you know you need to abandon.
Time-wasters need to go by the wayside, and true grit-and-bear-it-hard labor has to take its place.

Find a decent time management system and work it out.
There are numerous.
It's totally up to you which one you chose.
But if you don't want to become part of the 92% figure of individuals who fail to reach their long-term objectives, then you need to pay

attention to how you utilize the relatively little time you do have in this world.

What are the greatest techniques for managing your time?

One of the largest issues that most entrepreneurs have isn't only in how they can get enough done in such a demanding industry, but also in how they retain some kind of balance without feeling overly stressed.
This isn't simply about attaining and going for objectives around the clock.
This is also about quality of life.

Balance is vital.
If you lack balance in your life, you're going to feel stressed out.
Even if you're able to efficiently manage your tasks, without perfect balance you're going to ultimately hit your breaking point.
So, it's crucial to not just follow a system that will help you get things done, but also one where you prioritize personal and family time.

Don't forget to do things like take a stroll in the park or simply relax and listen to your favorite music with headphones on, or paint a painting, go on a date night, and so on.
That's more significant than you can imagine.
And when you do that, you attain some kind of equilibrium.
Life is brief.
So don't neglect such things as you seek your greater ambitions.
With that stated.

15 crucial time management tips for getting the proverbial job done.

1. Set goals the right way.
There are proper and incorrect methods to establish objectives.
If you don't appropriately establish your objectives, then you'll lack the necessary targets, which will push you to slip off course.
But when you position them the proper way, the sky's the limit.

Use the SMART goal-setting approach to help you see things through.

And when you do create those objectives, make sure you have tremendous deep-down reasons for wanting to reach them.

2. Find a decent time management system.

One of the suggestions for managing your time is to locate the correct strategy to accomplish it.

The quadrant time-management approach is perhaps the most effective.

It breaks your operations into four quadrants depending on urgency and priority.

Things are either urgent or significant, both, or neither.

Neither (quadrant 4) are the activities that you want to stay away from, but it's the not-urgent-but-important quadrant (2) that you want to focus on.

3. Audit your time for seven days straight.

Use seven days straight to analyze how you spend the time you do have right now.

What are you doing?

Record it in a diary or on your phone.
Split this up into chunks of 30 minutes or an hour.
What did you get done?
Was it time wasted?
Was it well spent?
If you utilize the quadrant method, circle or record the quadrant that the action was related with.
After seven days, add up all the numbers.
Where did you spend the most time?
Which quadrants?
The findings could startle you.

4. Spend your mornings on MITs.
Mark Twain famously observed, "If it's your job to eat a frog, it's better to do it first thing in the morning.
And If you must eat two frogs, it's advisable to eat the largest one first."
His point?
Tackle your greatest duties in the morning.
These are your most important tasks (MITs) of the day.

Accomplishing them will provide you with the largest momentum to help you sail through the remainder of the day.

5. Follow the 80-20 rule.

Another wonderful time management strategy is to apply the 80-20 Rule, often known as the Pareto Principle.

This rule states that 80% of the effort comes from 20 percent of the results.

In sales, it also suggests that 80 percent of the sales originate from 20 percent of the clients.

The trick?

Identify the 20 percent of the efforts that are producing 80 percent of the results and scale that out.

You can achieve this with rigorous monitoring and analysis.

6. Instill keystone behaviors into your life.

Charles Duhig poignantly invented the keystone habit in his book entitled, The Power of Habit.

In architecture, the keystone is the stone that keeps all other stones in place.

Similarly, keystone behaviors serve to not only encourage additional good habits but also aid to remove harmful habits as well.

Focus on keystone habits and you'll become much better at managing your entire time by making your habit-building a lot simpler.

7. Schedule email response times.

Turn off your email during the day.

When your email is coming in, it's easy to become sidetracked.

Schedule time to read and reply to emails.

If there's anything important, someone will phone or text you.

But when you have your email open, those distractions break your thinking flow and it's tougher to get back on track.

8. Eliminate bad behaviors.

One of the greatest time-wasters we have is our lousy habits.

Whether it's Netflix binge-watching, obsessively perusing social media, playing games, going out regularly to drink with pals, or so on, such unhealthy habits steal away the very little time that we do have.

Use your time wisely by eliminating your poor habits if you're serious about attaining major objectives in life.

9. Take frequent breaks when working.

One study suggests that you should work for 52 minutes and break for 17.

You might not have the luxury to do that.

But you should take frequent breaks.

If you're an entrepreneur working for yourself, this is vital.

It's easy to run on fumes and not even realize it.

Keep your mental, emotional and physical states at optimal levels by breaking often.

10. Meditate or exercise every morning.

You may not believe that this would assist you in better managing your time, but meditating and exercising every single morning provides you with balance.

Cut the pollutants out of your life and become serious by doing this and watch as your energy, stamina and mental concentration take a radical leap.

11. Make to-do lists in the evening for the following day.

Every single evening before bed, make a list for the next day.

Look at your goals and see what you can do to help move you closer.

This doesn't happen overnight.

It takes time.

But by making to-do lists, you're effectively setting goals for the day.

Daily goals are easier to achieve while helping to move us toward longer and bigger goals.

But that happens by creating to-do lists.

12. Find inspiration when you're feeling lackluster.

Resort to YouTube, TED Talks, and any other inspiring source you may turn to when you're lacking motivation.

It's hard to stay on track with your time when you lose that drive inside of you.

Find ways you can turn the fire back on by focusing on inspiring content and seeking out others who've achieved big goals.

13. Get a mentor who can guide you.

Finding a mentor is crucial.

It's easy to get distracted and dissuaded when you don't have someone guiding you.

But when you can personally rely on someone who's been through the wringer and can help you achieve your goals, it's easier to stay on track with your time.

Find a solid mentor that can aid you along your way.

14. Turn off social media app alerts.

Incessant social media app alerts aren't helping you with your time.

It's certainly harming you.

Turn them off.

You don't need notifications every instant or to know everything occurring with your buddies.

It's not important.

What's most important is to have some peace of mind and be better able to focus on the task at hand.

15. Declutter and arrange.

Studies have established that clutter in our surroundings encourages us to lose attention.

When we lose concentration, we lose time.

If you want to prevent it, declutter and organize.

Don't do it all at once.

Start small.

One drawer today.

A shelf tomorrow.

Maybe a closet the following day.

Just one each day.

You develop momentum and finally find yourself turning into an organizational warrior.

Chapter 2

Biggest check of life

If you're living paycheck to paycheck, that means all your money comes in and goes straight back out again before the end of the month.
That may not seem so horrible at first.
You're keeping on top of bills after all, right?
But if that's all you're doing, there's no way to look to the future—because you can't afford to save any money yet.
And there's no true security with your money now.
One tiny "life happens" incident might send it all tumbling down.

11 Ways to Stop Living Paycheck to Paycheck

1. Get on a budget.
Maybe you don't even know where your paychecks go.
Bills.
Payments.

Food.

You're simply keeping things paid and people fed.

It's time to start budgeting.

Why?

Because when you budget, you direct your money where to go instead of wondering where it went.

When you budget, you'll notice spending patterns you didn't even realize you had.

Then, you may make the adjustments you need so you can attain your goals—for now, and long into the future.

We can't repeat it enough: Budgeting is the cornerstone for all money management, and it's the first step in ending this paycheck-to-paycheck existence.

Don't put it off.

Get on a budget.

2. Take care of your Four Walls first.

When you're building up your budget, you'll jot down your income and then start deducting your spending.

What costs should you cover first?

The fundamentals, nicknamed the Four Walls.

The Four Walls are your priority, therefore make sure your money is set to pay for these items in this sequence before anything else:

Food\sUtilities\sShelter\sTransportation

After you take care of them, create a list of everything else you need to pay and handle it in order of priority.

When you run out of money, that's it.

You stop spending.

But by beginning with the Four Walls, you'll know you're keeping your family fed, your lights on, a roof over your head, and petrol in the vehicle to travel to work.

3. Start an emergency fund.

Let's speak about emergency finances.

Foremost things first, you need a basic emergency fund of $1,000.

You may question why the heck you need to save right now if you're busy simply trying to make ends meet.
But guess what?
Knowing you have this cushion between you and life will provide you with so much comfort.
It's your safety net for those "life happens" situations.

If you get into a bind, you may pay cash without thinking about which expenses you'll have to miss this month to cover things.
Listen: You certainly can save up $1,000—you simply have to make little (but conscious) daily, weekly and even monthly improvements.
And it will be entirely worth it.

4. Stop living with debt.
Okay, so here's the deal: Debt holds you back.
It's got you paying off last year's Christmas gifts in June.
And then you're left paying off that beach trip in December.

You can't get ahead like that.

And debt is growing sneakier and sneakier.
These days, installment payment organizations are on the increase.
They entice you at the checkout by stating you can pay for that French press in four simple installments.
Do you want to pour money into your expensive coffee machine for four months?
(No.)
Listen.
Living with debt (of any type) is one of the major factors keeping you in the paycheck-to-paycheck cycle.

Here's how:
First, quit taking on any form of new debt!
That means cease paying for stuff using a credit card.
Don't take out a new automobile loan.
Say "Heck no" to save 10% on that cardigan by signing up for a shop card, which will cost you in the long term.

Next, kick your debt to the curb by paying it off from smallest to biggest with the debt snowball.

Think of it like this: When you build your budget, how much of your money goes to debt payments every month?
That's how much more you'll take back when the loan is gone.
Goodbye, payments.
Hello, progress.

5. Sell goods.
Now it's time to bring in additional money!
One of the simplest methods to get your hands on some additional cash is by selling anything you can.
Maybe that's your jewelry, clothing, baby stuff, or even the additional automobile sitting in your garage.
(Yes, really!
At least think about it.)
Look, if you can part with anything and receive cash, do it!

You'll offer your bank account or budget some more padding, which is immensely beneficial when you're living paycheck to paycheck.

6. Get temporary employment or establish a side business.

If you've established a budget and sold some goods, but you still can just barely make ends meet, you may need a consistent means to raise your income.

Find a second job or side hustle.

Some wonderful choices for getting additional money include waiting tables, driving for Uber or Lyft, becoming a barista, working at a contact center, or signing up to be a substitute teacher.

There are also lots of work-from-home tasks you can accomplish after hours or on the weekend too.

Yes, it will be hard.

But this is just for a season.

Once you have some money in savings and debt out of your way, you may slow down again.

7. Live below your means.

This is crucial, so don't skip over it: Making more money will do you no good if you keep spending it all (and then some) (and then some).

Don't establish a side venture and keep living a lifestyle you can't afford.

If you aren't cautious, a raise in wages might make you spend even more money.

That's called luxury creep or lifestyle inflation.

All of a sudden, you can purchase things you couldn't before—and you could start turning quite loose with those purse strings.

Sure, it's tempting to spend more money while you're earning more of it, but don't do that!

Remember why you took on that additional duty in the first place.

Stay intentional, pay attention, and stick to your budget.

8. Look for items to cut.

If you're living paycheck to paycheck, now isn't the time to purchase T-bone steaks for supper, take a lavish trip, or visit your favorite restaurant.

This is the moment to decrease expenditures.
Look for any place in your budget where you may spend less.

Cut cable.
Call your internet and phone providers to decrease or cease your service for now.
Go to the library and parks instead of wasting entertainment money.
Stop eating out.
(Yes, we said it!)
We realize making compromises like this doesn't feel nice.
It hurts!
But keep telling yourself: This is not forever.
You're making temporary sacrifices.
It's time to put in the effort now so you can be in a better position in the future.

9. Save up for important purchases.

Nothing makes you anxiously out the minutes before payday more than if you recently squandered a ton of money on a huge buy.

So, if you sense anything approaching like you see the tread is becoming worn on your tires, save up and pay cash.

That way you're putting a little aside each month instead of wasting a whole month's budget.

Secondly, while you're living paycheck to paycheck, you shouldn't make nonessential major expenditures.

We discussed trips but think about the goods you know you want (but don't need) like that fantastic gaming system a buddy is selling.

Even if it's a wonderful offer, this isn't a terrific moment.

So simply say no.

10. Meal plan.
Food.

It's the first of those Four Walls, and you've got to eat.

But it's also a financial segment that may go out of hand if you aren't diligent.

When you create a meal plan, it'll help you avoid the temptations of the drive-thru since you know what's for supper back home.

Plus, you'll spend less on groceries when you know precisely what you need to purchase for the week.

No more random impulsive purchases or piles of fresh vegetables (purchased with good intentions but no plans) that end up rotting in the garbage!

You'll squander less and spend less, which frees up room in the budget and helps you move forward.

11. Remember your why.

Living paycheck to paycheck might seem like being locked in a revolving door with your money.

You're going around and around and never getting anywhere.
As soon as you decide you don't want to continue in circles anymore, you start all these recommendations and make motions.
It may be sluggish.
It can be challenging.
Some days you may want to give up.

Don't give up.
When things become difficult, remember why.
If it helps to think about the large future objectives you're working toward one day—traveling during retirement, paying for your kid's college tuition, or purchasing that property on the beach—then do that.

If you only need to look one step forward right now and envisage a life where there's no worry of overdraft fees or hearing your card has been denied, then concentrate on that.
Because it's coming.

Remember your why on that shift carrying groceries.

Remember why when you hold back from pushing "add to cart" even when you want (but don't need) the shoes.

Remember your why when you brew your coffee and bypass the barista.

Some days will be tougher than others.

And making such a significant adjustment in life will be challenging.

But you're tougher.

Chapter 3

Protecting your saving

Falling prey to fraud or having your assets stolen is especially distressing for the retired. How would you manage if you suddenly lost all of the cash you worked most of your life to accrue? With those funds gone, how would you ever be able to replace them? With limited time to repair your finances, you must take particular care of the assets and investments you have acquired for your retirement years.

Many of the scams aimed at the elderly typically utilize standard con methods. Making sure you are aware of the most prevalent techniques and frauds can assist you to avoid becoming a victim of fraud.

Be cautious about who you trust with your money
Cantonese has a saying: "Your children are not as good as your own money". While tragic, its connotation may be a terrible reality for many

older individuals, with stealing a widespread occurrence. All too frequently, it is the individuals nearest to you - friends, caretakers, and even spouses, partners, children, or other family members - who could swindle you out of your money.

There are several symptoms that everything may not be right with your money. Take notice of the following list and get quick treatment if you are anxious.

Money from your joint account is removed without your agreement.
Some of your property is sold without your consent and you never got any compensation.
Money or other valuables vanish from your residence.
You fear your signature has been faked or your seal has been used without your authorization.
You feel your will has been modified by someone else.
Your property or other assets are being exploited without your consent.

You have been intimidated or coerced into giving up money or property.

If you are afraid that someone close to you is exploiting your funds, get assistance quickly. This may be challenging if the issue includes family members and friends, who may be caring for you in your later years. If you - or any of your friends - are in this scenario, you have no option but to take action, putting aside anxieties about family scandals.

Wise techniques to care after your money
Your funds are there to sustain you through your retirement years and you need to take excellent care of them. With this in mind, there are a few things you should consider:

Manage your own money
Do not depend on other people to take care of your money, unless you are physically or psychologically incapable to bear such responsibilities. If you are afraid that your mind may no longer be up to it, you may commit your money to another responsible person by granting

them the Power of Attorney or by other comparable legal remedies.

Don't be greedy
Many conmen utilize the promise of enormous earnings as a technique of enticing others to invest. If you are greedy, fraudsters will find you easy prey.

Look out for fraud
Be watchful and mindful of traps and frauds that other older folks have fallen for.

Protect your personal information
Never give out data - including passwords and PINs - of your bank accounts, identification cards, ATM cards, or credit cards to anybody, no matter who they pretend to be.

Think carefully before you act
Be extremely attentive while examining financial offers or making new investments.

Always try to discuss it with someone you trust before you commit to anything.

Get assistance
If you suspect you have been fooled or feel you are the victim of theft, get assistance from the police or a social worker immediately.

Stick to Your Budget
Young couple putting up a budget online to add to their finances
This sounds so apparent, yet it is a basic fact. If you follow your spending plan each month and adhere to it, you will not dip into your savings account. If you do not have a budget, it is not unusual that you wind up borrowing a little here and there to pay necessities like food or energy bills. If you currently do not have a budget, set one up today. This is the greatest method by which you can obtain control of your spending and avoid dipping into your savings account. Checking in on your expenditures each day will help you stay within your budget.

Set Up an Emergency Fund

The unexpected does happen from time to time and you can end up with an expense that you have not planned for like three car repairs in six months. An emergency fund may help you handle these bills without delving into your savings for items like your house or your vacation. When you do use your emergency fund, you need to replenish it by adding money back into it over the next few months. This may mean slowing down your savings, but at least you are not pulling money from it.

Move Your Savings to Another Bank

When you are worried about overdrawing your account, it is easy to transfer money from your savings account into your checking account to cover it. While you should have your emergency fund easy to access like that, you may want to move your savings account to another bank where it will take more effort and more time to move the money. This can stop you from making impulse purchases and knowing that you have the money in savings to cover them.

Stop Using Your Credit Cards

It does not make any sense to be putting money into savings when you are using your credit card and carrying a balance. You are paying more in interest each month than you would earn in interest on your savings account. If you want to protect your savings, you need to clear up any credit card debt that you have. Make a plan to get out of debt today and stop carrying your credit cards with you, so you will not be tempted to use them.

Get Serious About the Way You Spend Money

If you are struggling to get by each month and dipping into savings because of spending, you can protect your savings by sticking to basic spending rules. There are several strategies you can employ including switching to cash for your shopping, couponing, and only buying things you need when they are on sale. Additionally, you might concentrate on minimizing your monthly costs to free up more money to handle your regular needs. The more proactive you are about how you work to save money on what you are spending, the more successful you will be at protecting your savings account.

Chapter 4

When things didn't go as planned

How to Adjust When Things Don't Go to Plan

Things didn't go as planned, and what do you do now?
Be patient.
Know that the situation can become better and there are options.
By learning to adapt, you may feel more in control.
Take the following steps to discover choices accessible outside of your initial goals.
Avoid concentrating on what went wrong and concentrate on how you can alter things for the better.

Keep your cool.
Take a minute to breathe and relax.
We all have barriers in life, and things don't always go as planned.
Avoid being harsh on yourself or others.

Getting furious will not make the issue any easier.

Take a step back for a minute.

Consider obtaining some distance from the scenario for 30 minutes, 1 hour, or a day.

Take a stroll.

Get a sip of water.

Distract yourself with something nice.

Try utilizing some self-soothing activities to help you calm down, such as listening to your favorite music, reading a book, or participating in a beloved pastime, such as knitting, playing guitar, or baking.

Come return to the problem when you're able to be patient and calm.

2. Acknowledge that you are dissatisfied.

Once you have calmed down, you may begin to address the disappointment.

The first thing you will need to do is to accept that you are feeling disappointed.

Try stating something like, "I am unhappy that things did not go my way."

You might also try writing about the disappointment.

What did not go your way?

Why is it troubling you?

How can you move forward from this disappointment?

Acknowledging your feelings allows you to process them and move on.

Avoiding or suppressing your feelings might feel good in the short term, but it will only make you feel worse later on.

3. Assess what went wrong.

Think about the problem from an impartial viewpoint.

Avoid blaming yourself or others.

Try to observe what occurred.

Your judgment may be influenced by bad emotions or stress.

Instead, listen to those that have a more objective opinion.

Take a neutral approach.

Your judgment should be based on the positives and negatives of the circumstance.
Evaluate both the good and the negative.
Consider putting out the advantages and negatives of the incident.

4. Accept what you can and cannot control.
Some things are just beyond our control.
For example, if you had plans to go for the weekend, and a storm arrives, things may not go as expected.
There are factors outside of oneself that impact and shape results.
Avoid dwelling on things that you can't change, and focus on what you can.
Think about how you can be a solution to a problem.

5. Learn to adapt.
Adaptation is crucial when things go bad.
It is part of our development as humans to learn to adapt to our situations.

The more flexible you are in your plans the more likely your expectations of what you desired will be satisfied.

Life is not a straight and simple route.

It is loaded with twists and turns.

Each day we are learning how to adjust to our everyday lives and problems.

For example, think about how you go to school or work.

While there may be one exact method you achieve things, consider the countless alternatives accessible.

Some routes may be easier and shorter, others may be longer or more difficult.

But they still arrive at the same destination.

Assessing Your Options

Explore what your expectations were.

Sometimes we feel irritated when things don't go according to plan because they don't satisfy our expectations.

Think about the expectations you had for the circumstance.

Think about whether your expectations may have been too severe or restrictive.

One strategy or goal is not a measure of your value.

Just because things didn't work out this time, that doesn't mean they will never work out in the future.

For example, you and your friends wanted to go to a special restaurant, and you find out it's closed.

You may be disappointed or upset because you were expecting a nice meal there.

Instead of assuming that the only decent dinner is at this one restaurant, analyze the other locations accessible.

2. Restate your aim.

Since your initial strategy hasn't come through, return to your original purpose or aim for the issue.

You undoubtedly have brainstorming statements about your aims and aspirations.
Go back to that time.
Talk about your aim again with everyone involved.

Consider writing down your initial intention.
Putting the situation in writing, particularly for bigger plans, can help to solidify what your goal is.

Use this goal as a framework to restate and reimagine your alternative plans.

3. Think about the options available.
So your original plan hasn't worked out?
Now is the time to consider the various choices accessible.
What is your Plan B or Plan C?
If you don't have an alternate strategy in place, then analyze additional choices to explore.

Gather information about various choices available.
Consider writing down the alternative possibilities available, and generating a list of pros and disadvantages.

Reassess the techniques and probable outcomes of your plans.
Talk with those engaged in the process—friends, family, and co-workers.
See if they may have more suggestions.

While these alternatives may not be your initial concept, one or more of them may come up as excellent as the original.

4. Choose future measures.
Take action.
Be explicit about future measures you're taking.
Avoid feeling dejected, as if the initial idea was the best or the only one available.
Approach this following step feeling cheerful and hopeful rather than negative.

Be confident in your selection after you've analyzed the many possibilities accessible.

Coping with Change

1. Build resilience.

Having resilience implies that you can keep working toward your objectives even if things do not go your way.

Building this talent requires time and effort, but it may assist you to endure disappointment more quickly.

To create resilience, you can.

Put things into perspective.

When things do not go your way, assess whether it is worth investing time and energy in.

For example, if you had hoped to receive a job that you interviewed for and did not get it, then your time and energy could be better spent looking for new positions.

Take a minute to put your circumstances into perspective to assist you to build up your resilience.

Maintain excellent connections.

If you have solid connections, then you will probably feel more comfortable when things do not go your way.

Try to keep solid ties with your friends and family to feel more comfortable through challenging times.

Challenge unhelpful notions.

Resilient individuals may modify their thoughts to help themselves remain motivated and to continue working towards their objectives.

You may do this too by confronting notions that are inaccurate or hurtful.

For example, if you catch yourself thinking, "I will always fail," then you may dispute this inaccurate and destructive belief.

Try telling yourself something like, "Things may not always go my way, but if I keep working towards my objectives then I will attain them."

2. Use the past for guidance rather than regret.

The past is exactly that, the past.

While you can't take back what has occurred, you may utilize this experience as a beneficial tool.

Think about the best and the worst of the situation for you or the people you care about.

What can you or others learn from this

For example, let's imagine you're working on an important project with a small team.

Maybe the project is more than intended, and more time demanding than you thought.

So the team ends up racing to finish the project and it feels to you like the project is failing.

This might be a chance to recognize when to seek further aid.

Maybe you and the team could take a different approach to the project.

Maybe the project isn't as bad as it seems because you had too high of expectations.

3. Avoid giving up.

When something doesn't go the way you'd like, you may feel like you've failed.
Avoid seeing yourself with hate, and instead, focus on what you are thankful for.
Resilience is crucial to keeping oneself motivated.

Giving up means giving in to your self-doubts.

Reframe your negative thoughts by focusing on the excellent things that have transpired.
Even if they are minor things.

For example, if you were expecting to obtain an A on a test and instead got a C, think about how you may look at the wider picture.
Maybe this is your only C on a test this semester?
Maybe this isn't the only test for the class so you may study more for the remaining exams.
Maybe the other students all got Cs on the test too?

4. Learn from errors.

Life is trial and error.
Some mistakes are our own, and some are those of others or simply forces beyond our control.
Own up to your mistakes, but avoid dwelling on them.
When you are honest with yourself, then you can learn to grow and become better.

Mistakes are learning opportunities.
They may push you to the unseen edges of what's possible and what's not.

When you try new things, you may make mistakes.
This is part of life.
It can make you stronger and more prepared for the next time.

Consider staying to yourself, "I realize that I screwed up, but it's not the end of the world" or "I can learn from this.
I can be better.
I can be ready for the next time."

5. Ask for help.

There's no shame in asking for input.

Talk with people that you trust about what they think about the situation.

Get guidance from a range of individuals.

Seeking guidance might make you feel less alone with your ideas or problems.

People on the outside could have a better vantage point on what's going on.

Chapter 5

Simple step to make life easier

HOW TO MAKE LIFE EASIER

To be honest, I have a hectic life and not a lot of free time on my side.
No amount of simplification can wave a magic wand over my life and make it stress-free or a stroll in the park.
I guess it goes for pretty much all of us at some point or other!

Life may become hectic, and extremely busy and it's not always of our making.
There are so many more elements that come into play.
Work, family, financial or health issues, things to do, and places to be…

All we can truly do is find a balance, simplify our life wherever feasible, and make purposeful judgments on what supports us and what doesn't.

They may not all be perfect for you, but it's potentially a beginning place to help you analyze your own life.

Take what you can, adjust what you desire, and utilize what appeals to you and fits with your present season of life.

Even simple steps and minor modifications may have a tremendous effect over time...

15 WAYS TO MAKE LIFE EASIER

Here are some tips to make daily living simpler.
Try them out for yourself and discover which works for you!

1. Simplify your finances

Money is a necessity and managing it wisely is always a good thing.

For some of us, managing our money can be stressful.

We can be struggling to pay bills, suffering from debt, or simply can't get our minds around mathematics.

Make it simpler for yourself to remain on track with your money by streamlining your accounts. Create a monthly budget to keep on top of your monthly income and outgoings

Check your bank statements against receipts regularly

Set up bills to be paid automatically by direct debit

Make a plan to deal with any debt

Put money aside for savings if you can spare it

Shop wisely

2. Declutter your home
For many of us, home is where the heart resides and it's the focus of family life.
Sometimes, however, houses are more a source of worry than pleasure.

A messy house is a drag on your time and energy.

Too many things will make your house harder to maintain and longer to clean.

None of these things are likely to make your life easier!

Have a look around your home now and see if you can streamline a few things.

Do you love everything in your home, do you need all that stuff and does it add value?

Or does it just serve to muddle your home and muddle your mind?

Take some tiny measures to declutter an area or room in your house and you'll quickly see and feel the advantages — more space, more time, more freedom, and less stress.

Make your life easier at home with these 6 tips to help you start decluttering or these 20 ways to declutter your home for real impact!

3. Stop putting things off

Sometimes we are our own greatest adversary and I've fallen into this trap myself many times! Putting things off seldom solves anything and in my experience, it frequently only makes a matter worse and stresses me out in the process.

Either we can't make a choice, we're anxious about the eventual outcome or we get caught weighing the advantages or best means of doing things.

We strive for perfection and end up becoming immobilized into inactivity.

When you have an issue, deal with it.

If you've got something to do, take action.

Feeling stuck and don't know where to start? Just select a location and dig in.

If you have a problem, list the pros and drawbacks and follow the outcomes.

Procrastination is terrible for you!

It freezes us in our tracks as we merely get caught up in the problem and never take action or fix it.

Be a doer and an action-taker rather than a procrastinator!

4. Be intentional with your time

When many of us claim that our life is too complex, what we truly mean is that we're too busy.

If you can discover methods to be less busy then maybe life could seem a bit simpler.

Being less busy isn't always simple to do in regular daily life.

The key to making it work for you is to be purposeful about your time and what you say 'yes' to in the first place.

Here are some ideas for you to try:

Look thoroughly at your schedule and delete any events or obligations that no longer serve you, bring value to your life, you or your family have outgrown, and/or those you no longer like.

Factor in some spare time each day to relax and simply go with the flow.

Could you wake up earlier and utilize this time to get things done that you can't accomplish throughout the rest of the day?

Or what about spending 20 minutes in the evening preparing your luggage, meals, or clothing for tomorrow, so you don't have to do them in the morning?

Be mindful of your time and use it wisely.

5. Define your priorities
Have you thought about what your genuine priorities could be?
Not simply the ones that yell out from your diary or To Do list.
A new automobile or a larger house?
Or would it be making your kids giggle or seeing them ride a bike without aid for the first time?

Take time to establish your genuine priorities in life and enjoy the inherent worth of the smaller things in life.

Jot down in a notepad the people, events, places, and experiences that mean the most to you.

Make a deal with yourself to attempt to do something each day to respect those priorities

6. Plan and prepare

Planning and preparing for what's ahead can undoubtedly help make life simpler.

Be less prone to forget things

Know what has to be done and when

Foresee and avert any difficulties before they come up

Some of us are better at planning than others.

If you find it difficult, just remember that it doesn't have to take ages and the time you've saved planning can more than cover the time you waste dealing with the fall-out of not being prepared!

For example, imagine missing a birthday and then having to make a special journey to the stores for a present and card when you could have bought this last time you were at the shops anyway?

Make life easy and perform some frequent forward-planning:

Check your calendar weekly (and preferably daily) so you know what's happening

Keep a visual To Do list on paper or your phone so you know what you need to do.
Don't depend on keeping this knowledge in your brain where you're likely to forget it!

7. Get organized
Putting processes and procedures in place so you're usually more organized, efficient, and productive may make life simpler and easier.

Some examples may be:

Regular weekly meal-planning and grocery buying,

Filing systems for papers and vital documents and spreadsheets to monitor your expenditures.

Locate a good 'home' for everything from hats and gloves to toys and DIY equipment so you can find everything quickly and effortlessly.
It also helps prevent those dreaded clutter hotspots!

For organizational and productivity advice check out this article on 25 ways to be more organized.

8. Set explicit targets
Do you ever make goals for yourself and then wonder why you never attain them?
Perhaps you fly it through life without really knowing where you'd want to be in 5 years, much alone next month?

Only then to wonder where the time has gone and why haven't you saved that money, purchased that property, pursued that training, and so on?

Simplify the process and accomplish things in life that you want to do without becoming side-tracked by the irrelevant.

Check out my article on how to make goals and accomplish them for additional assistance with this!

9. Establish housekeeping habits

Running a house may be a big drain on your time and your energy.

Cleaning, washing, tidying, sorting.

Everything has to be done even if you don't feel like it.

Make life easy and put some regular home habits in place.

A little amount done regularly is significantly easier on your time and energy!

Your house will operate on auto-pilot and free you up to go on with the rest of your life!

10. Declutter your clothing

Do you have enough things in your closet but yet can't find something to wear each morning?

Make things simpler by decluttering your wardrobe.

Remove everything that doesn't fit, you don't wear, or is ruined.

You'll be left with outfits that you adore and a few fewer things to sort through.

Deciding what to wear in the morning will be so much faster and simpler!

11. Make peace with yourself

Accept yourself for who you are and what you have.

Stop trying or wishing to be somebody different.

Spend on improving your own life rather than being jealous of others and you'll discover your life will be a lot simpler!

12. Look after yourself

It doesn't matter if you can steal simply 5 minutes or 5 hours.

Take some time each day to do something for yourself (a bath, read a chapter of a book, make a cake, and so on) (a bath, read a chapter of a book, bake a cake, and so on).

Recharge your batteries with a little time for yourself and life will seem a little simpler, even if it's not!

13. Put limits in place

Avoid spending your time and energy on activities that don't provide value or aren't vital.

Stop saying yes to things you don't want to do.

Don't waste time doing something when you'd rather be doing something else.

Don't allow one-sided relationships and friendships to consume your energy.

It is difficult enough to make life easy by putting in place boundaries.

Make some big judgments about what you'll accept into your life and what you keep out and this will eliminate some of the little, minute decisions you make every day.

14. Identify the major source of your stress
Is there one thing in your life that causes you a lot of stress, upset, or overwhelm?

Maybe it's body confidence and you'd like to lose weight?

Not enough time for yourself or time in general?

A friendship that's a touch one-sided?

A work that's going nowhere or isn't flexible enough for your family life?

Choose just one item that's making you depressed and develop a plan to deal with it this week.
Next week, select another or expand on the one from the week before.

15. Take frequent exercise

Taking regular exercise is a crucial means of keeping your body and mind strong and healthy.

It doesn't have to be difficult, simply a daily stroll in fresh air or some moderate stretches are acceptable.

Listen to your body and move it as much as you can.

Chapter 6

Three-weeks plan to transform your life

Change, particularly the good sort, is not an easy undertaking.

There are a great number of components involved in each given part of life, and there are sufficient of these aspects as it is.

Well, Dave Brailsford, a trainer of the elite British cycling team, Team Sky, reasoned that given the fact that there are hundreds of minor factors, one may improve a little amount in each one to create a huge overall difference.

He claimed that by the accumulation of marginal benefits, it is feasible to overrun the competition after a period.

Making tiny 1% changes in things ranging from the comfort of the seats and weight of the tires of your car to the most comfortable pillows that allow athletes to get better rest, yielded impressive overall results – it took only 3 years for Sir Bradley Wiggins to become the first ever Brit to win the Tour de France.

By adapting this basic but very successful strategy of aggregation of marginal benefits to our own lives, we may start making a tremendous change in under a month.

The principle is really easy - every day for the next 21 days you will make a little and manageable 1% alteration to a certain element of your life, which will result in the establishment of 21 excellent habits that you may keep practicing for years and years.

All the adjustments are minor and easy to adopt, however, after a few years you will be miles from where you are today in terms of physical and mental health, productivity, and general quality of life.

Day 0 – Make a solid choice right now
We all want to start things at the beginning of the week or the beginning of next month, but you should sit down right now and commit to the program.
Make a solid determination to start implementing these little changes first thing tomorrow.

Day 1 – Drink a couple of glasses of soda less
Pouring out coke\sLooking at the manufacturer's official website we see that a can of Coca-Cola contains 139 calories, and most sugary drinks are roughly the same.
The can holds less soda than two average-sized cups.
That implies that by drinking merely a couple of glasses fewer you are cutting down on over 150 calories and 40 grams of sugar a day, resulting in extremely moderate, but consistent weight

reduction assuming other parts of your diet stay about the same.

You may drink extra water instead.

Day 2 – Go outdoors and walk for 30-40 minutes
An hour of walking at a regular steady speed can burn between 200 and 300 calories, depending on your weight size — bigger persons burn more calories during the same workout than skinnier ones.

This means that 30 minutes will burn 100-200 calories.

It's not that tough to find the time for a short walk, and you can even split it down into 2-3 walking sessions of 10-20 minutes over the day.

Combine that with fewer drinks and you get roughly 250-350 calories fewer per day without altering anything at all.

Day 3 – Eat a fresh salad before lunch and supper
You don't have to replace your usual meals with salads, just make sure you eat a medium-sized

bowl of fresh salad — lots of vegetables and no toppings except spices and olive oil – before lunch and supper.

Not only do you obtain enough much-needed vitamins, but the fiber in the veggies will also help you feel full, so you won't be able to overeat bad and extremely calorie meals as much.

Day 4 – Read 10-20 pages of a novel

It has been demonstrated time and time again that reading offers lots of psychological and even mental health advantages.

Not to mention that it makes you more eloquent and broadens your viewpoint.

Even if you are a slow reader it won't take you more than roughly 30-60 minutes to read 10-20 pages.

Do this every day and you'll be getting through at least a book or two every month.

You can start with some of them.

Day 5 – Start doing bodyweight workouts

Getting a solid exercise in doesn't take anything except goodwill and 20-30 minutes of spare time.

You may practice this sort of bodyweight training 2-3 times a week to get some fantastic health advantages, acquire a sexier physique, and enhance your confidence.

Day 6 – Warm up your body and stretch in the morning

Doing 3-5 minutes of jumping jacks or mountain climbers as you get out of bed is a wonderful method to warm up your joints and it gets the heart circulating.

You may follow this with about 10-15 minutes of static stretching.

You may do them after your exercise on your workout days instead of in the morning.

Stretching offers several health advantages and is pretty simple to accomplish.

Day 7 – Devote 30 minutes to master a new skill

There are certainly a handful of abilities that you would want to have right now.

Whether it's business-related, general skills that can be used for a wide variety of things like team management or dispute resolution, we could all benefit from learning something new.

By committing only 30 minutes a day to mastering a new talent you will have acquired the fundamentals and be reasonably proficient at it within a few months.

Day 8 – Replace one of your normal snacks with fruit and nuts

We grab snacks several times throughout the day, whether it's because we're a little hungry, upset, or simply bored.

The next time you feel like you need a snack, reach for a couple of apples, a banana, a pear, or a cup of berries, combined with a handful of walnuts or almonds.

Nuts have been shown to reduce cholesterol levels and can lower the risk of heart disease, while certain berries have great amounts of antioxidants, and various fruits contain plenty of vitamins, minerals, and fiber.

It's a healthy snack and it keeps you feeling full for longer.

Day 9 – Get some vitamin D and fish oil supplements

In a perfect world, we would have access to all that the body needs, but this is not the case.

Most people lack omega-3 fatty acids in their diet – these keep the heart healthy, the skin looking young and your mind sharp – and hardly get enough sun exposure, which limits vitamin D production which is responsible for bone density and keeping normal testosterone levels.

These supplements are relatively cheap and will ensure that you stay healthy despite common dietary deficiencies.

Day 10 – Use moisturizer after you shower, shave, or wash your face

Keeping your skin as soft, smooth, and elastic as possible is the key to looking and feeling young even as you get older.

A lot of people, particularly men, fail to utilize moisturizers regularly.

This means that after washing your skin will dry out and even become flaky, becoming less soft and smooth over time.

By using a good moisturizer regularly you will ensure that your skin becomes fresh and soft, and remains that way for a long time.

Day 11 – Do 10-15 minutes of running/cycling/jump rope training

If you've committed to the improvements you've made, you will already be walking a little more, warming up and stretching, and performing a couple of brief exercises a week.

However, to maintain optimum cardiovascular health you will need to boost your heart rate and hold it in an elevated condition for a set length of time.

You don't have to be precise about it – as long as you perform some jogging, cycling, or jump rope exercise for approximately 10 minutes 2-3 days a week you will dramatically minimize the risk of heart disease.

Day 12 – Brush and floss your teeth after supper and before bed
An essential though often ignored element of overall wellness is your dental health.
Tooth decay may create a range of difficulties, acute pain being one of them, and can cost you a lot to fix if things get out of hand.
A lot of food gets trapped in your teeth after heavy meals, and the germs do the greatest harm if you fail to brush before bed and let them eat away at your teeth overnight.
With this easy practice, you will have a gorgeous smile for a long time.

Day 13 – Listen to some calming music and perform breathing exercises for 10 minutes after work
Listening to music on the sofa

Once you arrive home from work it's time to swap mental gears from busy and stressed to comfortable and relaxed.

Music is a wonderful stress reliever and when paired with some effective breathing techniques may help you quiet down and relax your body and mind pretty fast.

Just 10 minutes of this soothing treatment a day and you will become considerably calmer and happy in the approaching months.

Day 14 – Do one activity that's a touch outside of your comfort zone

The greatest approach to learning and improving is to move slightly beyond your comfort zone.

You can't simply do this with everything all at once, but doing one tiny activity that you don't feel that comfortable with - speaking to a crowd, singing, etc – every week can make you grow more comfortable with it and ultimately help you conquer your fear of it.

Focus on one thing until you are comfortable and then transition to something else.

Start modest – e.g. speaking to five people – and move to something huge with time – e.g. presenting a toast at a celebration.

Day 15 - Start a discussion with at least one random person throughout the week
A lot of situations in our everyday lives might be uninteresting and even a little embarrassing.
By chatting to a stranger while waiting in line or seating in a coffee shop you may truly feel happy.
Connecting with people puts boredom at bay, letting you vent your problems and get a few good chuckles.
Approach one random person a week and initiate a discussion - who knows what intriguing places that will lead you.

Day 16 – Get a foam roller and massage your muscles for 5 minutes before bed
Foam rollers are a terrific technique to give yourself a thorough massage and reach all the tense muscles.

A myofascial release, e.g. easing up those tight knots in the muscle, is accomplished, which will lessen muscular discomfort, enhance mobility and help you feel calmer.

You may do it a few minutes before a workout or before going to bed to relax and prepare for sleep.

Day 17 – Watch 15-20 minutes of TED speeches every other day

TED presentations provide you insight into several diverse subjects, may inspire you, make you think, and like with literature, extend your worldview.

Here are some of the more popular ones that you may listen to every other day, or if you have a chance, even one each day.

Learning about diverse subjects will come in very basic pieces, but will increase over time and even drive you to conduct some more study on your own, thereby obtaining lots of information over time.

Day 18 – Read about body language and work on yours throughout the day

Spend an hour or two on the weekend to do some study on body language and then attempt to improve yours at different times of the day.

You want to have the body language of a confident and strong person, to know which errors to avoid, and understand other people's intentions to a degree.

With time you will be able to demonstrate confidence and become more forceful, detect whether someone likes you or doesn't like you by reading minor queues, and much more.

Day 19 – Take your lover someplace pleasant after the week or treat yourself to a good night out

It is crucial to maintain your connections healthy, and if you don't have a significant other it is necessary to find yourself, someone, you can be close and personal with.

By taking one day out of the week, or even just once in two weeks if you're busy, and dedicating it to the other person you will gain a lot of goodwill with them.

On the other hand, if you are single, go out and have some fun.
Get a few buddies to come with you and attempt to meet some new people - some of that confidence, expertise in striking up a conversation with strangers and good body language could come in help.
This can help you reduce tension and keep your relationship healthy or help you overcome the fear of rejection and enhance your love life.

Day 20 – Shut off all the lights and electrical devices before retiring to bed
Lack of sleep is a typical issue in the contemporary world and it may have several bad side effects.
There are a lot of things that might keep us distracted like computers and phones, but we also infrequently establish appropriate sleeping settings.

Your room ought to be black when you go to sleep – no music, background movies to assist you to dose out, simply a couple of additional YouTube videos or lights of any type.

If you make this a habit, you will progressively begin to have more regular sleep patterns and sleep for the full 7-9 hours that you need to feel well-rested, focused, and energetic.

Day 21 – Take the day off from a humdrum routine and grab some peaceful time for yourself\sWolf relaxing in a field

Once or twice a month designate a day to be your leisure day.

Distancing yourself from daily problems and other people and just doing nothing can do a whole lot of good for you.

It might be a weekend in the countryside, a fishing trip, sitting around the home watching a full season of your favorite program, or whatever else enables you to get some quiet and relaxation.

A fully relaxing day or two like that per month would go a long way towards improving your mental and physical health, which may be significantly deteriorated by stress.

Slow and steady wins the race
If you follow this complete advice and make a little lifestyle adjustment every day for the following 21 days, you will end up with several extremely beneficial habits that may help you make a large overall improvement in terms of health, fitness, productivity, relationships, and happiness.
It's all about staying with these tiny improvements for the long haul and slowly improving over time.
At one time you'll look back and be shocked at how great of an effect these 1% improvements have made.

www.ingramcontent.com/pod-product-compliance
Lightning Source LLC
Chambersburg PA
CBHW070320220526
45465CB00013B/1746